CANDLEWICK PRESS

FIND OUT ABOUT
Animal Camouflage

illustrated by

Martin Jenkins   Jane McGuinness

Some animals are very good at hiding. Often they hide to try to
escape from animals that would like to eat them, but sometimes they
hide from animals that they would like to eat. Hiding by blending
in is called camouflage. Here are some of the animals that use
camouflage—a few of them have tricks that might surprise you . . .

These animals look like leaves.

When its wings are folded, the oakleaf butterfly looks just like a dead leaf.

Leaf insects are usually green with brown spots and jagged edges that look as if another animal has been chewing on them.

The leaf mimic moth also looks exactly like a dead leaf.
Its wings even look like they're curled up the way leaves often are.

So does this one.

You could easily mistake an African Gaboon viper for a heap of dried leaves on the forest floor. Don't step on it, though—it has a very venomous bite! It lies quietly in wait, and when a prey animal walks past, the viper strikes with its fangs.

These animals look like twigs.

The coloring of a peppered moth caterpillar
can slowly change to match its surroundings.

Peppered moth caterpillars turn into moths.
The moths have great disguises, too, blending in
with the bark on tree trunks.

So do these.

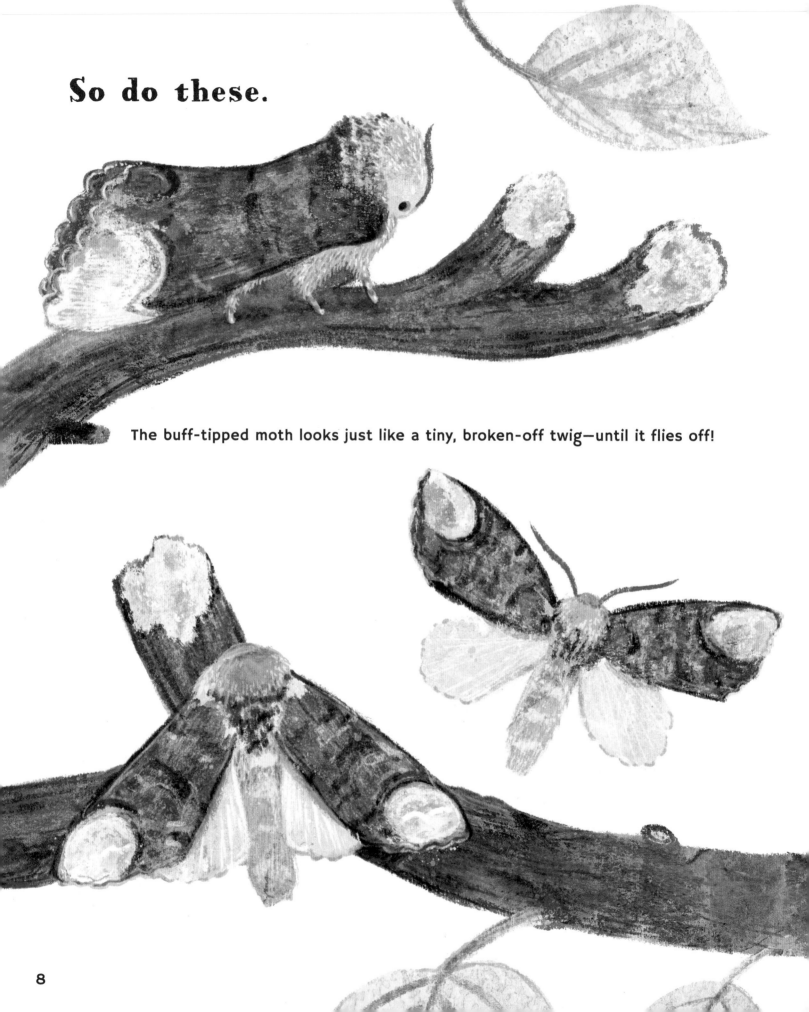

The buff-tipped moth looks just like a tiny, broken-off twig—until it flies off!

8

Stick insects don't usually fly. There are lots of different kinds. The largest can grow to more than 12 inches (30 centimeters) long—the longest insects in the world.

This animal looks like a flower.
Watch out—it might bite!

The flower mantis hides among bunches of brightly colored flowers, keeping very still. When a small insect it wants to eat flies past, the mantis lunges out and grabs it with its strong front legs.

And this animal looks like a tree stump.

The frilled lizard spends
a lot of its time on tree
stumps. Its dull brown color
allows it to blend in well,
making it hard to see.

But look out . . .

It might give you a fright!

If the lizard is suddenly alarmed—by an eagle or snake,
for example—it opens its mouth wide and spreads out its frill,
making it look much bigger and scarier than it actually is.

These animals hide in the desert.

spotted sandgrouse

Many animals that live in deserts, like sandgrouse and gerbils, have sand-colored feathers or fur that makes them hard to spot.

horned lizard

The scaly patterns of many
desert lizards match the pebbles
and small stones in their natural habitat.

gerbil

And these animals hide in the ocean.
Some can even change color!

ghost pipefish

peacock flounder

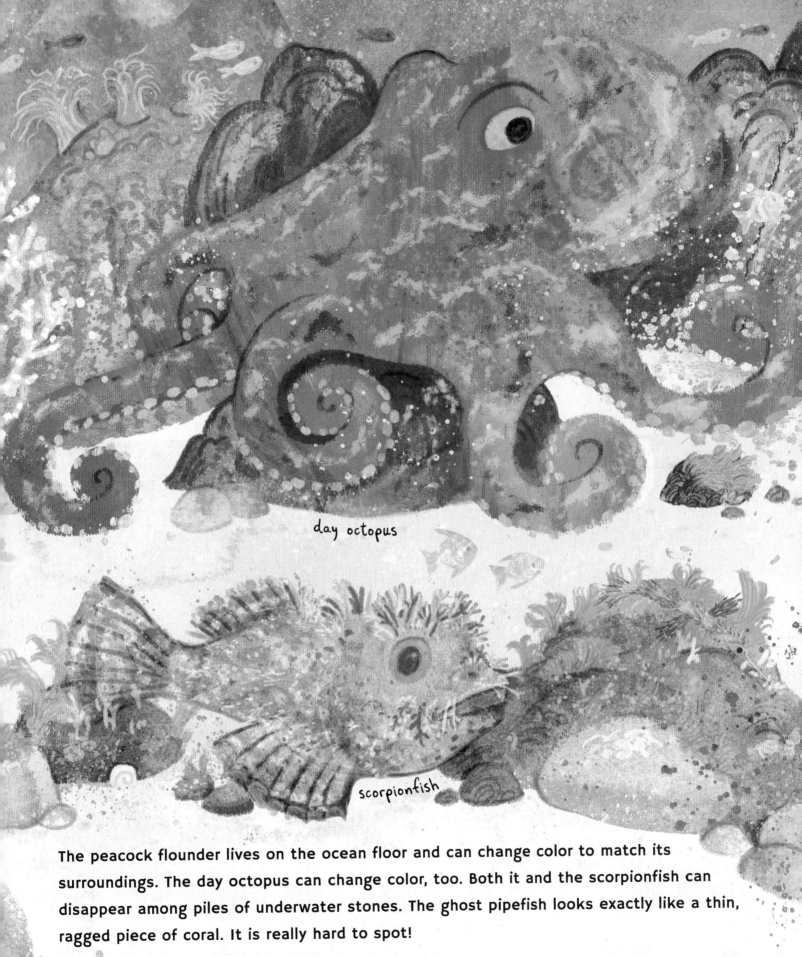

day octopus

scorpionfish

The peacock flounder lives on the ocean floor and can change color to match its surroundings. The day octopus can change color, too. Both it and the scorpionfish can disappear among piles of underwater stones. The ghost pipefish looks exactly like a thin, ragged piece of coral. It is really hard to spot!

These animals hide in the snow.

Arctic hares

ptarmigan

Ptarmigans grow white feathers in winter, which keep them well hidden in the snowy places where they live. Arctic hares and Arctic foxes usually grow white fur in the winter, too.

Arctic fox

But these animals don't try to hide at all.

monarch butterflies

poison dart frogs

Poison dart frogs release deadly poison from their skin. Many are brightly colored as a warning to other animals to keep away. Monarch butterflies taste horrible. Other animals recognize their markings and don't try to eat them.

The harmless scarlet king snake looks very similar to the deadly coral snake. This similarity helps keep the scarlet king snake safe from other animals, who wouldn't want to mix the two of them up!

scarlet king snake

coral snake

It's their way of saying, "I'm scary! Keep away from me!"

More About Animal Camouflage

Animals that use camouflage usually look like things in the places where they live: rocks and soil, for instance, or parts of plants, like leaves and bark. They have patterns and colors that match their surroundings really well, making it hard for other animals to see them. They spend a lot of time staying very still, as they are much easier to see when they move.

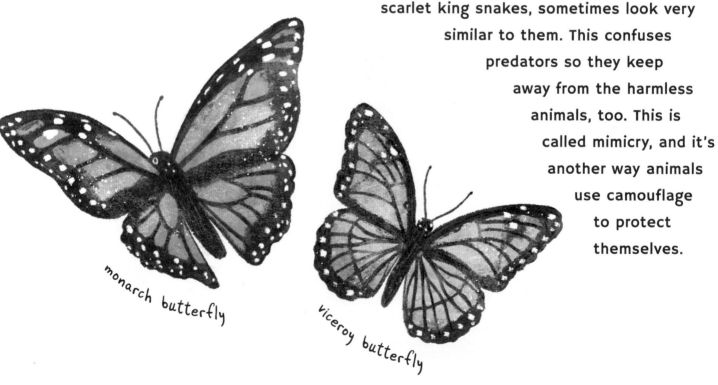

Some dangerous or poisonous animals, like venomous coral snakes or nasty-tasting monarch butterflies, have bright colors to warn other animals to keep away. Harmless animals, like viceroy butterflies or scarlet king snakes, sometimes look very similar to them. This confuses predators so they keep away from the harmless animals, too. This is called mimicry, and it's another way animals use camouflage to protect themselves.

monarch butterfly

viceroy butterfly

INDEX